P9-CJI-862

TEST YOUR LATERAL THINKING IQ

✦ ✦ ✦

Paul Sloane
Illustrated by Brett Barlow

Sterling Publishing Co., Inc. New York

Books by Paul Sloane

Lateral Thinking Puzzlers (1991)
Test Your Lateral Thinking IQ (1994)

(with Des MacHale)

Challenging Lateral Thinking Puzzles (1992)
Great Lateral Thinking Puzzles (1994)

Edited by Claire Bazinet

Library of Congress Cataloging-in-Publication Data

Sloane, Paul, 1950–
    Test your lateral thinking IQ / Paul Sloane ; illustrated by Brett
Barlow.
        p.   cm.
    Includes index.
    ISBN 0-8069-0684-7
    1. Thought and thinking. 2. Lateral thinking. 3. Lateral
thinking—Testing.   I. Title.
BF441.S62   1994
153.4'3—dc20   94-12348
                                                                     CIP

10   9   8

Published by Sterling Publishing Company, Inc.
387 Park Avenue South, New York, N.Y. 10016
© 1994 by Paul Sloane
Distributed in Canada by Sterling Publishing
% Canadian Manda Group, P.O. Box 920, Station U
Toronto, Ontario, Canada M8Z 5P9
Distributed in Great Britain and Europe by Cassell PLC
Villiers House, 41/47 Strand, London WC2N 5JE, England
Distributed in Australia by Capricorn Link (Australia) Pty Ltd.
P.O. Box 6651, Baulkham Hills, Business Centre, NSW 2153, Australia
Manufactured in the United States of America
All rights reserved

Sterling ISBN 0-8069-0684-7

*I would like to thank the following
people for their help on this book:
Ajaz Ahmed, Carole Frazer, Des MacHale,
Rick and Pat Squires, and Phil and
Delia Stimpson.*

*I also want to express my gratitude
to my wife, Ann, and daughters Jackie,
Katy, and Hannah for their encouragement.*

Contents

Introduction

✦ ✦ ✦

Lateral thinking is now recognized as an important and necessary force for change. It is a significant personal skill which can enable us to solve problems at home or in business. At a national or international level, it may be the only way to overcome the seemingly insoluble problems of our society and to manage the changes we need.

This book explains what lateral thinking is. It helps you to test and expand your powers of lateral thinking in a way which is fun rather than hard work. The lateral-thinking process is explained and there are practical problem-solving exercises which permit the assessment of your skills in each part of the system. As you work through the book you will be able to see your skills in the application of lateral thinking improve.

Lateral thinking is not an obscure or arcane skill; it is a latent power which everyone has. It can be developed through training, requiring only a change in mental attitude and an open-minded approach to problem solving.

The exercises in the chapters that follow require the help of a colleague or an assistant who acts as adjudicator. You start by selecting a problem. The adjudicator, knowing the solution to the problem, then answers your questions as you try to figure it out. The adjudicator's answers can only be "yes," "no," or "irrelevant" (or he or she can ask you to restate the question if it is particularly difficult to answer in that form). The more quickly you solve the problem (i.e., the fewer questions or clues that you need), the higher your score.

The scoring system and the assessments that follow each chapter are not claimed to be precise. They are based on experience and are for general guidance only. There is an element of luck in solving the problems and a puzzle which one person finds easy may well stump a friend and vice-versa. The assessments are based on the scores from five puzzles, which is too small a sample to give a truly reliable indication. However, choosing five puzzles in a section gives two people the chance to take turns as adjudicator and problem-solver and to assess their skills in a reasonable time.

The whole process is designed to be fun and to sharpen your skills at the same time.

Good puzzling!

The Need for Lateral Thinking

✦ ✦ ✦

An Early Example

The ancient Greeks built a magnificent and prolific civilization. They excelled in many fields of human endeavor from science to philosophy to sport. Their architecture was splendid, with many fine temples and inspiring buildings. Yet, in all their marvellous constructions remaining today, one never sees an arch. Their architecture, like that of the Egyptians, Incas, Aztecs, and other ancient civilizations, was based on upright columns supporting beams, called lintels, on which higher floors or roofs were placed. This limited the size of the buildings and the open spaces and spans therein because the column and beam approach has limited strength.

The invention and use of the arch changed architecture completely. Some stonemason had the vision and insight to use an arch of stones to carry a load. Each stone was shaped like a wedge and they slotted together

(without mortar) to form a shape with much greater intrinsic strength than the column and lintel. This development allowed the creation of much larger and more magnificent buildings with open space and light.

Although the Greeks knew of the existence of the arch, it was the Romans who used it to magnificent effect. It enabled the construction of huge, graceful aqueducts and of buildings with beautiful domes and vaults. The unknown stonemason who had the courage and foresight to design buildings with arches rather than columns and beams was a true lateral thinker. That breakthrough transformed architecture and the buildings in which we live.

What Is Lateral Thinking?

The term lateral thinking was coined by Edward de Bono to describe a kind of thinking which is different from conventional or normal thought. In conventional thinking (or what is sometimes called vertical thinking) we move forward along familiar lines using experiences and assumptions from similar situations. At each stage we build on the progress, the logic, and the assumptions which we have used before. We believe that we use a logical and rational approach.

However, sometimes this process no longer serves us. It reaches limits that we can only overcome by throwing out our core assumptions and by approaching the problem from a completely new angle, i.e., by thinking laterally. Conventional thinking in ancient Greece meant that the construction of larger temples was limited by the size and strength of columns and lintels. A completely new design of curved lintel, the arch, was needed to achieve real progress.

A major limitation for the Romans was their numbering system, a system in which 9 was represented by IX and 16 by XVI. As a counting system this was workable, but for multiplication, factoring, fractions, or any kind of advanced numerical calculation it was hopelessly inadequate. The system which replaced it came from the Arabic civilization. It was built on a completely different concept and introduced a radically new idea—the inclusion of zero in numbers. The Roman numbering system did not incorporate zero in its higher numbers but the Arabs gave us a system which allowed 0, 10, 100, 1000, and so on. Nearly all the subsequent development of Western mathematics, science, and engineering depended on this change. Probably the greatest contribution which the Arabic world gave us was nothing—the symbol 0!

The point of the story is that no amount of development, extension, or adaptation of the Roman system, a system used throughout a huge empire, could have made it an adequate tool for the demands of science. It required an utterly new method of numbering—a lateral development.

At the beginning of the nineteenth century, it was believed that the only way for man to travel faster was to breed faster horses. Yet no attempts, however inspired, to breed swifter horses or to build more effective carriages could achieve the real breakthroughs which first the steam engine and then the internal-combustion engine delivered.

It is natural for us to keep doing things the conventional, proven way rather than to reassess or reframe the whole problem. Everyone assumed that the sun and planets went around the earth until Copernicus, in 1543, asked the question, "What if we look at the whole universe from a different perspective? What if we put the sun at the center rather than the earth?" By deliberately taking a different perspective on the situation, Copernicus was able to construct a much more realistic model of the solar system, one with the sun at the center rather than the earth.

At the beginning of the twentieth century, Albert Einstein did something similar when he asked his famous question, "What would the world look like if I rode on a beam of light?" By looking at the world from a completely different perspective he was able to show that all the conventionally held wisdoms about the absolute relationships governing time and space were not accurate. He showed that the properties of an object were not absolute but were relative to the position of the observer. The passage of time is relative. For example, if there were identical twins and one rode off in a high-speed rocket while the other stayed on earth, then the one who returned from his rocket ride would find that his brother had aged more than he had.

But we should not assume that lateral thinking is an obscure technique for scientists, architects, and inventors. It can be usefully applied in many other fields. We all take supermarkets for granted but they were a very radical idea when first introduced. Previously, shops always worked on the principle of assistants serving customers. Most shops were small and personal enterprises but they were costly and offered a limited choice. The man who is credited with revolutionizing our approach to shopping is Michael Cullin who, in 1930, set up the first of the King Kullen chain of supermarkets. His idea was to turn the concept of shopping around and to let customers serve themselves from a very wide selection of goods. The consequences to the retail trade of this simple notion were enormous. Over the next half century, thousands of small shopkeepers were driven out of business by more efficient and appealing chain stores offering huge self-service selections. Out-of-town shopping centers replaced main streets lined with small shops.

We can use lateral-thinking techniques to solve problems in all walks of life—in business, in education, in our social life, and within our family. Whenever conventional methods of problem solving are proving inadequate we should try thinking laterally as a way to come up with fresh solutions and creative new approaches. We then have to carefully select a new type of solution and implement it. The problems in this book are training in the use of lateral thinking to come up with unusual ideas and solutions. The selection, testing, and implementation of solutions is discussed in brief in the final chapter. For the moment we need to concentrate on the basic methods of problem solving using lateral thinking.

The Elements of Lateral Thinking

There are four key elements in the process of lateral thinking for problem solving. They are:

1. *Testing assumptions* In approaching every new problem or situation we need to ensure that we are open-minded. We have a natural tendency to assume all sorts of things which may or may not apply and therefore we tend to jump to the wrong conclusions. When we approach a problem carrying the wrong mental baggage we immediately block out all sorts of possible solutions.

2. *Asking the right questions*   It is said that the art of management is knowing which questions to ask. This is also true in lateral thinking. In order to solve problems laterally we have to start by asking very broad questions to establish the correct framework of the problem. We then use more specific questions to sift information, test hypotheses, and arrive at a solution.

3. *Creativity*   In order to solve a tough problem we often have to use an unconventional approach. If our standard problem-solving procedures do not work, then we should be creative and approach the issue from an entirely new direction. Instead of tackling the problem head-on, we have to approach it from the side, laterally. The ability to be imaginative in approaching problems is a key skill in lateral thinking.

4. *Logical thinking*   Lateral thinking is more than just coming up with wacky ideas. We need the ability to logically analyze those ideas with the cold precision of the surgeon's scalpel. Without the disciplines of logic, reasoning, analysis, and deduction, lateral thinking would be no more than wishful thinking. But whereas conventional thinking starts with experience and logic, lateral thinking uses them to refine creative solutions.

We will explore each of these key elements in more detail in the chapters that follow.

How the Puzzle Tests Work

✦ ✦ ✦

Rules for the Tests

In order to practise lateral thinking and to assess progress in each component skill there is a series of puzzles to be solved. Each of the next four chapters contains a number of these problems and they should be attempted not on one's own but with the help of a friend or colleague who acts as adjudicator. Of course, you can also act as the adjudicator for your friend, child, colleague, etc. The adjudicator needs a watch, a pencil, and some paper.

The aim is to work out the right answer to the puzzle with the least number of questions, and wherever possible to make questions result in "yes" answers. This will lose you fewer points and lead to a higher score. If you get stuck you can ask for a clue, but they cost you additional points.

The following rules apply in tackling the problems:

a. You must have with you an adjudicator who knows

the solution to the puzzle and answers your questions.
b. Do not attempt a puzzle if you already know the answer; for example, if you read it while browsing through the book. If you already know the answer, then it makes the assessment pointless.
c. The adjudicator can only answer "yes," "no," or "irrelevant" to your questions (or ask you to restate your question if it is ambiguous or likely to mislead).
d. For the first two minutes you can ask as many questions as you like without any penalty.
e. After two minutes the adjudicator deducts points for questions. One point is deducted for every "yes" answer, two points for every "no" or "irrelevant."
f. You should choose five and only five of the problems for the formal assessment. The higher the initial score of the problem, the harder it is considered to be.
g. Your score on each puzzle is the initial score reduced by your deductions for questions and clues.
h. The logical puzzles section does not require an adjudicator and does not involve questioning.
i. Although there is no formal time limit, if you are stuck on any puzzle after half an hour, then you should give up and score 0.

Choose puzzles which are new to you—if you know the answer to a puzzle, then it cannot be one of your five. If you are feeling confident and want to go for a higher score, then choose the higher-scoring puzzles. (Score values are given at the beginning of each puzzle.)

Clues should not be offered lightly. In general, a clue should only be given when the questioner has had a good try but has become baffled and needs help to get going again. Where there is more than one clue they should be given in the sequence in which they are arranged. However, the adjudicator can use some discretion with the clues. For example, if the questioner has already figured out all the information given in the first clue, then the adjudicator can go straight to the second clue. If you want to make the whole process a little easier, then you can agree between you that the adjudicator can invent his own clues if appropriate. However, this and any other changes to the rules would invalidate the assessment process.

Scoring

You start with the score associated with the particular puzzle. After the initial two-minute, free-questioning period, for each question you ask which results in a "yes" answer the adjudicator deducts 1 point. For each question which results in a "no" (or "irrelevant") answer the adjudicator deducts 2 points. If you get stuck, then the adjudicator can give you one of the clues, in which case a certain number of points associated with that clue is deducted. You can then ask more questions or ask for more clues until you solve the puzzle. Your score is then assessed as in this example:

Original Puzzle Score	80
Less 25 Questions with "Yes" Answers	−25
10 Questions with "No" or "Irrelevant" Answers	−20
One 10-point Clue	−10
Final Score	25

If you cannot solve the puzzle, or you ask so many questions, or need so many clues that your final score reaches 0, then you score 0. You cannot record a negative score.

The aim is to figure out the answer to the problem as given in the answers section, not to come up with any plausible answer. In many puzzles it is possible to postulate an alternative solution which meets all the initial conditions. If you do this, then "Well done"—but you have not solved the puzzle. You need to establish the solution stated in the answers section. Generally that should be the "best" (in the sense of most apt) solution, but sometimes lateral thinkers come up with truly lateral alternatives! If so, please send them in—but keep trying to find the book solution.

The higher the score associated with each problem the more difficult it is to solve. You should attempt five problems. It is fine for you and your colleague to take turns as questioner and adjudicator. When looking up the answer to a puzzle you should, of course, try to avoid reading the answers to other puzzles!

1
Testing
Assumptions

✦ ✦ ✦

We Assume Too Much

There is an old saying that to assume "makes an ASS out of U and ME." In approaching situations and problems, whether lateral-thinking puzzles or everyday challenges, we all tend to make too many assumptions. We assume that the situation is like other situations we have experienced before and so we blind ourselves to all sorts of possible solutions.

Of course, it is natural to make assumptions. If on a walk in the woods we saw a brightly colored snake, we would assume it was poisonous and avoid it. It might or might not be poisonous but our assumption places us in a least-risk situation.

However, there are many occasions when the natural assumption that things will proceed the conventional, proven way is dangerous. In the 1930s the British and French military high commands approached the problems of German aggression using conventional techniques. They assumed that any new war would be like the First World War but fought with better equipment.

They therefore prepared their defenses against an assumed German frontal attack by using the much superior fortifications of the Maginot Line along the Franco-German border. This solution proved completely inadequate. The German high command redefined the basis of modern warfare by introducing the new concept of "blitzkrieg." Using fast-moving armored divisions and some lateral thinking, they did the unthinkable and swept through neutral Holland and Belgium into an undefended section of France. The magnificent and expensive Maginot Line of defenses was bypassed and France was defeated.

Marconi, the inventor of radio telegraphy, faced many cynics and doubters as he developed the theory and practice of radio transmission. In 1901 he proposed to test sending radio signals across the Atlantic. The experts all scoffed at the idea. Because radio waves travelled in straight lines they assumed that radio signals could not go around a curved surface like the earth. Experience and logic supported that assumption, but Marconi dramatically proved it wrong when he successfully transmitted a signal from England to Canada. Un-

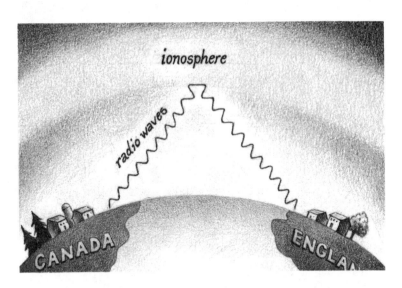

beknownst to all the experts, there was an electrically charged band, the ionosphere, which reflected the radio beams back to the earth.

We all suffer from the mental restrictions of too many assumptions. We may laugh when we hear the joke about the alien who came to earth, went up to a gasoline (petrol) pump and said, "Remove your finger from your ear and take me to your leader!" But what assumptions would *we* make on seeing a new creature? It is said that when the North American Indians first saw a man riding

a horse they assumed that this was some new animal with two heads, two arms, and four legs.

There is an old riddle which goes like this: "A blind beggar had a brother who died. What relation was the blind beggar to the brother who died?"

If you ask ten people this question they will most probably all give the same answer: "Brother." But that is not the answer. The answer is that the blind beggar was the *sister* of her brother who died. This puzzle, like many others, works because the listener or reader invariably makes a false assumption: that a blind beggar must be a man.

Assumptions Blind Us

Making assumptions is a natural but lazy habit. We assume that a new situation is similar to previously experienced situations. This saves us time; we do not check out all the details surrounding the situation but immediately jump in with an answer. Although this process will sometimes help speed things up, it will inevitably screen us from other possibilities and options. Often we will leap to the wrong conclusion and miss the chance to make a better decision.

Many puzzles work because they contain ambiguities. We often go forward on a route based on a simple misunderstanding of an ambiguity. Once we embark on that route it is very difficult to solve the problem—for example, if we assume that the blind beggar is a man. Try this poser. You have exactly $101 in your pocket. You have just two notes and no change. One of the notes is not a $1 bill. What are they?

Most people struggle with this little conundrum because they are misled by an ambiguity in the wording. *One* of the notes is not a $1 bill. That is correct—it is a $100 bill. So the solution is the simple one of a $1 bill and a $100 bill.

Ambiguities occur not just in puzzles but in all walks of life. Whenever someone speaks we make all sorts of assumptions about his or her meanings. It is easy to misinterpret any ambiguous statements to fit our own preconceived views. Consequently, we often jump to entirely the wrong conclusions because our assumptions are erroneous. Before making a serious judgment about a person or decision in a situation, we should check out the assumptions on which we have based our assessment. We will sometimes find that the inherent ambiguities in the case have misled us.

Let us go back to the snake, which we always assume to be dangerous. It was recently reported that a Brazilian car thief used an ingenious method to steal cars. He would slip a brightly colored but harmless snake through the open window of any suitable car that stopped at a set of traffic lights. Invariably the terrified driver would leap out of the car to avoid the assumed threat. The thief would then calmly get into the driver's

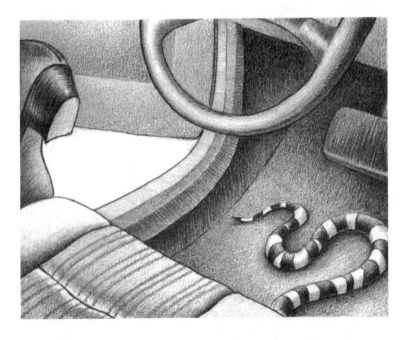

seat and drive off in the car. He exploited the fact that people will almost always assume that an unfamiliar-looking snake is poisonous.

In tackling the next batch of problems, be sure to carefully check out all the assumptions that you made when you heard the problem. Test your assumptions by asking simple questions. Restate the puzzle in a slightly different way to see if your statement is still correct. Most of these posers are very simple once you drop all your false assumptions, but that is not always easy to do.

Skill Test 1

1.1 The Secretary's Daughter   POINT VALUE/50

A woman went to visit her bank manager and she took her young daughter with her. The bank manager said that the woman's daughter could stay with his secretary during the meeting. When the woman and her daughter left, the secretary turned to another secretary and said to her, "That little girl was my daughter." How could that be?

1.2 Pizza   POINT VALUE/50

A man walked into a take-away pizza parlor. He ordered one deep-pan pizza with cheese, tomatoes, and double anchovies, one crispy pizza with asparagus, cheese and tuna, one house special with extra cheese, two portions of onion rings, a diet cola with ice, a diet cola without ice, a water, and an orange juice. The woman behind the counter served him and then said, "You are a plainclothes police officer aren't you?" The man was indeed a plainclothes officer. He had never been in the pizza parlor before and the woman didn't know him and had never seen him before, so how did she know what he did?

1.3 The Fishermen's Riddle   POINT VALUE/50

An old riddle tells the tale of two fishermen who returned one day and made the following statement: "The ones we caught we threw away. The ones we could not catch we kept." What did they mean?

1.4 The Barber Paradox　　POINT VALUE/50

In a town in ancient Greece there was a law stating that all men must be clean-shaven and that no man might shave himself. The only person allowed to shave people was the licensed town barber (who was forty years old). There was only one barber. Since the barber was bound by the same law, who shaved the barber?

1.5 Late Arrival　　POINT VALUE/60

A father was speaking to his teenage daughter. "You arrived very late, at 3 o'clock in the morning, and you kept me and your mother up waiting anxiously for you. I do not want that to ever happen again."

"But, Father," the girl replied, "I will never be able to do that again." What did she mean?

1.6 Watch That Movie　　POINT VALUE/60

Hugh had never seen the movie "Top Gun" before he got on the transatlantic flight to take him from London to Los Angeles. However, he had heard that it was good and was pleased to see that it was due to be shown during the flight. After lunch, "Top Gun" was screened, but Hugh did not bother to watch it even though he had a clear view of the screen and the sound and picture quality were fine. Why not?

1.7 The Cabin　　POINT VALUE/70

In the mountains there is a cabin. Inside, three people lie dead. The cabin is locked from the inside and there is no sign of a struggle or of any weapons. What happened?

1.8 The Unkind Cut　　POINT VALUE/70

A man deliberately cut off some of his fingers and one of his ears. Why?

1.9 The Triangles Death   POINT VALUE/70

A man was found shot dead outside a bar. Around him were 52 triangles. Why?

1.10 The Soldier   POINT VALUE/70

During World War II a German counterattack freed one of their countrymen who had been besieged by Russian partisan fighters. He greeted his liberators, asked if he could borrow a gun, and then shot himself. Why?

1.11 The Bird   POINT VALUE/70

A man saw a bird on a tree in his garden and he immediately knew that he had lost something of value to him. What was it?

1.12 The Bank Manager   POINT VALUE/70

A bank manager was on his way to work one day. He was wearing a mask. Why?

1.13 The Fish   POINT VALUE/80

A man saw a fish, and because of that he shot himself. Why?

Clues

Each clue costs 10 points.

1.1 The Secretary's Daughter

1. This does not involve adoptions, step-parents, in-laws, or grandparents. The little girl was the secretary's daughter and she was the daughter of the woman who visited the bank manager. That is all you need to know.

1.2 Pizza

1. There was no visible sign from the man's appearance, speech, or mannerisms that he was a police officer. The assistant deduced it from his order.

2. The assistant had heard that same order before.

1.3 The Fishermen's Riddle

1. They were not talking about fish. But they were talking about other creatures which were unwelcome.

1.4 The Barber Paradox

1. The barber did not break the law. There was no beard, moustache, or whisker on the barber's face, yet that face was not shaved by the barber. Check all your assumptions about the barber!

1.5 Late Arrival

1. All the statements were correct. The father was not angry. He was teasing his daughter. The girl could not arrive in that fashion again because what she did can only be done once.

2. The statements made did not refer to the previous night or any recent night.

1.6 Watch That Movie

1. He wanted to watch the movie when he got on the plane but not when it was shown after lunch. Nobody had ruined the movie for him by telling him the plot. He had nothing particularly interesting to do after lunch. He had a perfect view of the screen.

2. This has nothing to do with the lunch or the plane or anyone else on the plane. It has everything to do with the timing of showing the movie after lunch.

3. He watched the movie.

1.7 The Cabin

1. All three died at the same time. Their deaths were violent but accidental.

2. They knew they were going to die immediately before they died. They died because they were in the cabin. If they had gotten out of the cabin three hours earlier they would have lived. If they could have gotten out three minutes earlier they would still have died.

1.8 The Unkind Cut

1. He did this deliberately to deceive certain people.

2. The man was imprisoned at the time he did this.

1.9 The Triangles Death

1. The number 52 is very significant.

2. He had been playing a game—a very serious game.

1.10 The Soldier

1. He shot himself because he could not live with himself knowing what he had just done.

2. He had his own rifle but no ammunition in it.

1.11 The Bird

1. The bird was a large but not particularly rare bird. The type of bird is important.

2. The bird had taken what he had lost but he could not

now get it back from the bird. What he had lost was something he had recently bought at considerable expense.

1.12 The Bank Manager

1. He had a very long journey to work.

2. He was not trying to hide anything. He was trying to exclude something—but not something you breathe.

1.13 The Fish

1. The fish was sent to him.

2. The fish was a signal.

3. He knew that he was bound to die.

Test 1 Score

Add your scores for the *five* problems you tried. Then assess yourself against the following:

Grade A   Over 250 points—an excellent score
You are open-minded, versatile, and imaginative. Better still, you are able to check your assumptions and discard the false ones. This will stand you in good stead to handle new situations with creative approaches and effective new solutions.

Grade B   201 to 250 points—a very good score
You are more imaginative than the average person and are quite flexible in your approach. But occasionally you cling to initial assumptions too long. Now that you have seen how making the wrong assumptions can blind

you to certain answers, you should focus on checking all prior ideas and being really open-minded in tackling problems.

Grade C   141 to 200 points—an average score

Like most people you tend to approach problems with preconceived notions that sometimes prevent you from seeing new and effective solutions. Try to be more open, adaptable, and receptive to new ideas. Go over the puzzles that you found difficult and analyze what it was that blocked your progress. You will probably find that you were sometimes too rigid in your approach and clung to initial assumptions for too long.

Grade D   Less than 140 points—a below-average score

You definitely need to loosen up and be more flexible in sounding out these problems. Go over the puzzles that you found difficult and analyze what it was that blocked your progress. If you had difficulty thinking of appropriate questions, then the next section will help. If you stuck strictly to your initial assumptions in each puzzle, then it is a clear sign that you need to be much more open-minded and flexible. Be prepared to question everything that you have taken for granted about each new problem or situation you encounter.

2
Asking the Right Questions

✦ ✦ ✦

The Questioning Technique

The directors of a famous but struggling pen-manufacturing company focused on answering one key question, "What can we do to increase sales of our pens?" They tried all sorts of specific answers and ideas but sales continued to fall. Eventually they recruited a new marketing director. He started by asking a different and more fundamental question, "What business are we really in?" He found that people bought their expensive pens as gifts for others rather than as pens for themselves. The answer to this question caused the company to change its pricing, packaging, distribution, etc. They changed their orientation from being a pen company to a gift company that sold pens. They became much more successful.

It is very important in facing any problem to ask questions before selecting possible solutions. But asking any old questions will not do; we have to ask the right questions. Very often the right questions are fundamental questions. This is particularly true at the beginning of any investigation. We should establish the broad framework first and home in on the detail later. So in opening a sales negotiation we would not ask, "If we reduced our price by ten percent, would you order?" A better initial question would be, "What are the main things you are looking for in selecting a product and supplier?"

Similarly, if I asked you to guess a number I had selected between 1 and 100, your best initial question would not be, "Is it 37?" A better question would be, "Is it less than 50?" If the answer to that question is "yes," then your next question could be "Is it more than 25?" and so on. With this binary-selection technique you can always find out my number in no more than seven questions. With the rifle-shot "Is it 37?" approach you have a one in a hundred chance, and it will take, on average, 50 questions to guess the answer.

Many people use just such a rifle-shot method in tackling lateral thinking problems. They try to guess a specific solution to the problem each time. It is much better to ask broad questions that narrow the field of enquiry. So instead of "Was she shot by a jealous former lover?" we would do better to start with "Was she murdered?" and then "Did a man kill her?" etc. It is for this reason that the scoring system rewards "yes" answers and penalizes "no" answers by imposing a higher cost for "no" answers. A rifle-shot question will generally result in a "no" answer. A broad question will often produce a "yes." Indeed, it is possible to construct your questions to increase your chances of "yes" answers. If you only suspect early on that the subject of the puzzle might be a one-legged dwarf, then do not ask the rifle-shot question, "Was he a one-legged dwarf?" (Answer: "No.") It would be better to test the hypothesis with a broad question. Since you suspect that he is disabled, you could ask the broad question "Does he have any kind of physical disability?" (Answer: "Yes.")

In the next batch of problems, as you check your assumptions and move to the solution, be sure to start with broad questions that eliminate whole areas of investigation. Home in on the underlying reasons for what happened. Do not simply gather facts, but try to establish the motives involved. Why did people act the way they did? What changes or motivations were at work? Once you have established the broad framework of what happened, then you can move in to find out the specific details. Try to get "yes" answers and do not use specific rifle-shot questions unless you are super-confident.

Skill Test 2

2.1 Luigi's   POINT VALUE/50

Luigi's is an excellent restaurant with a fine reputation. However, one day all the people who had lunch there were sick. There was nothing wrong with the food. What happened?

2.2 What a Drive!   POINT VALUE/50

A golfer in the United States took a club from his golf bag and hit a drive so that the ball travelled through four states. How did he do this?

2.3 Tall Buildings   POINT VALUE/50

A well-respected Japanese insurance company has many offices around the world. All its offices are at least ten storeys high and the company insists on taking at least a ten-storey building even if it does not need all that space. Why does it do this?

2.4 The Broken Bag   POINT VALUE/50

A healthy woman died because the plastic bag she was carrying broke. There were many people around her at the time but they were completely unharmed. What happened?

2.5 A Veiled Threat   POINT VALUE/60

A woman wearing a veil was grabbed by two complete strangers and thrown into a swimming pool. Although she was a strong swimmer, she died. Why?

2.6 The Unexpected Kiss   POINT VALUE/60

A healthy man was surprised and delighted when an attractive woman whom he had never seen before came up to him in the street, threw her arms around him, and gave him a long kiss. They were unknown to each other before this meeting. Why did she do it?

2.7 The Legacy   POINT VALUE/60

A man received an envelope in the post. Inside it there was another envelope which contained only a letter. The letter said, "Here is the $20,000 I promised you. Best regards, Dad." There was no cheque or cash but the man was perfectly satisfied. Why?

2.8 By the Pool   POINT VALUE/60

A man was lying dead next to a swimming pool. There was a towel around his face. How had he died?

2.9 The Fisherman   POINT VALUE/70

A keen fisherman lived near a large lake which contained many fine fish. He fished from his motorboat. He would travel all along his side of the lake in search of fish, but he would never go to the southeastern part of the lake, even though the fishing there was good and it was within easy reach of his boat. Why did he never go to that part of the lake?

2.10 Food for Thought   POINT VALUE/70

The Danish government issues all the staff in one government department free biscuits every morning. Why?

2.11 Cheap Treasure   POINT VALUE/70

A man acquired an item without choosing it specifi-
cally. It was not of particular value to him, but a second
man offered him $5,000 for it as he wanted it as a gift for
his wife. The wife was delighted with her present, but
within a week she damaged it. This was not a problem
as a replacement was easily made at a cost of $20. Some-
time later the wife reluctantly sold it to another woman
for $8,000. What was it?

2.12 The Train Problem   POINT VALUE/70

John and Bill were brothers who lived in the same
house. One day they were returning from town by train.
Bill missed the train which John caught and had to wait
for the next one. They both alighted at the same station,
though, of course, Bill's train arrived later. (Both trains
travelled at the same speed.) Both men walked the same
distance home and walked at exactly the same speed.
Yet they arrived home at exactly the same time. Neither
dawdled nor paused for any reason, nor used any means
of transport other than train and walking. What happened?

2.13 Lost Jewelry   POINT VALUE/80

A couple went on holiday for three weeks. They carefully locked their house. When they returned, the wife
was distressed to learn that because there had been a
power failure she had lost all her fine jewelry. Why?

Clues

Each clue costs 10 points.

2.1 Luigi's

1. There was nothing wrong with the food, the drink that was served, or the atmosphere. The people eating lunch were normal, healthy people. Other people eating lunch at other places that day were fine. It was not something they saw. The problem was caused by the location of Luigi's restaurant.

2.2 What a Drive!

1. He was a regular golfer with no special skills. He stood on the ground and hit the ball, which then travelled through four states before coming to rest. No one else touched the ball after he hit it, and no additional speed or energy was imparted to the ball in any way.

2. The ball did hit something and was deflected.

3. The four U.S. states are big states, including Arizona and Colorado.

2.3 Tall Buildings

1. This has nothing to do with the company's products, name, or advertising, but it has to do with the company's philosophy.

2. The company does this with its employees in mind.

2.4 The Broken Bag

1. The woman was travelling on a plane when this happened.

2. The plastic bag contained drugs.

2.5 A Veiled Threat

1. She died accidentally. The two strangers had tried to save her.

2. She wore the veil because of the work she was carrying out prior to the accident.

2.6 The Unexpected Kiss

1. Both the man and the woman were in perfect health. Neither was famous. She was not rewarded for kissing him.

2. She thought that she recognized him.

2.7 The Legacy

1. There was no secret or coded information passed in the letter or envelope.

2. There was an outer envelope, an inner envelope, and a letter. Yet the man had received something worth $20,000.

3. The outer envelope was new and had the man's address on it. The inner envelope was old and had someone else's address on it.

4. The address on the inner envelope was not of someone known to either man.

2.8 By the Pool

1. He had died as the result of an accident. No one else was involved in his death. His death had nothing to do with swimming or drowning.

2. He had placed the towel around his face prior to his death in an effort to help him survive.

3. If he had reached the pool he would have lived.

2.9 The Fisherman

1. His reluctance to go to the far side of the lake has nothing to do with fishing.

2. There is no physical barrier across the lake. However, the fisherman is acting rationally in not going there. There is a danger to the fisherman in crossing to the other side of the lake.

3. Other people do cross the lake safely. Under certain circumstances the fisherman could also cross safely. He would need to get permission.

2.10 Food for Thought

1. The biscuits are not for the staff's own consumption. They give them away.

2. They give the biscuits away for their own protection.

2.11 Cheap Treasure

1. In this puzzle the relationships between the people do not matter. What matters is that this particular item, while useful to many, is very valuable to one woman but not to another.

2. This particular item can only be used in conjunction with a larger item, but it can be bought and sold separately. The items in general are very common and inexpensive, but this particular one is rare and valuable.

3. It is valuable only to a small number of women sharing the same name.

2.12 The Train Problem

1. John caught one train and Bill the next train. They

both arrived home at the same time and walked at the same speed over the same route. It follows that they both left the station at the same time. John's train arrived first and he immediately started walking. Bill's train arrived later and he immediately started walking.

2. They were large, fast trains carrying many passengers. The gap between the trains was only two minutes.

2.13 Lost Jewelry

1. She was not robbed. Her jewelry was lost by accident.

2. She had hidden the jewelry in what she thought was a very safe place.

Test 2 Score

Add your scores for the first *five* problems you tried. Then assess yourself against the following:

Grade A   Over 250 points—an excellent score
You are a first-rate questioner who can ferret out the truth with a minimum of questions even in difficult and strange situations. Have you considered a career in detective work? Seriously, if you can combine your questioning technique with an open-minded, imaginative, and logical approach, then you will be a superb lateral thinker.

Grade B   201 to 250 points—a very good score
Your questioning technique is good and in time you can get to the answers. With more practice you will learn to focus even better on the key issues and will therefore need fewer questions.

Grade C   141 to 200 points—an average score
If you solved the puzzles but used too many questions, then you need to practise your questioning technique. You probably wasted too many points on questions that led down blind alleys. Concentrate on establishing the basics first, and then reduce your field of questioning to focus on the most promising line of inquiry. If you failed to solve the puzzles at all, despite lengthy questioning, then you probably need a more imaginative approach. This is the topic of the next chapter.

Grade D   Less than 140 points—a below-average score
The comments above apply here, too. You should go over some of the puzzles which stumped you and, knowing the answers, try to think of the sorts of question that would have helped you solve them. It is much easier to think of the right questions once you know the solution, and this procedure can help you to develop your questioning technique for other problems. Then keep practising on new puzzles to improve your ability to ask the right questions.

3
Creativity

✦ ✦ ✦

The Leap of Imagination

Let us imagine that you could have taken a competitor
or observer from any Olympic Games before 1968 and
whisked them forward in time to watch a modern Olympic Games. The one event which would truly amaze
them would be the high jump. Until 1968, every high
jumper "rolled" over the bar with his or her face down.
In 1968 an American, Dick Fosbury, introduced an entirely new approach, the "flop," leaping over with his
back close to the bar and his face up. Fosbury was
ranked 48th in the world in 1967; yet in 1968 he caused
a sensation when he won the Olympic Gold Medal with
his unprecedented technique and a leap of 2.24 metres.
What he introduced was in two senses a leap of the
imagination, and it revolutionized high jumping. Now-
adays, nearly all the top jumpers use his method.

Very often, to solve a problem we have to do more than refine or improve current techniques. We have to introduce an entirely new concept. This approach is the very essence of lateral thinking. Let us look at some historical problems and how a leap of the imagination was used to solve them.

• The problem of how to provide buildings with adequate lighting was not solved by bigger or better candles but by the invention of the electric light bulb.

• The problem of how to give individuals a faster means of personal transport was not solved by breeding faster horses but by inventing the motor-car.

• The problem of how to make aircraft maneuverable was not solved by refining the plane but by inventing the helicopter.

• The problem of how to make a better and easier fastener was not solved by further developing the button and buttonhole but by the invention of a completely different device, the zipper fastener. An even more lateral solution to the same problem was created by the invention of Velcro.

In each case above, progress was achieved not by conventional improvement of existing solutions but by completely new and different approaches. This is the crux of lateral thinking: achieving practical new solutions by moving towards the problem from a new direction rather than by trying to continue to develop old and proven methods.

John Sculley's autobiographical book, *Odyssey*, describes his years as president of the Pepsi-Cola Company and then as president of Apple Computer, Inc. In it, he tells of the major problem that Pepsi had in combating Coca-Cola's "trademark," the distinctive hourglass-shaped bottle. It represented a massive marketing advantage, it was known worldwide, and it was a company logo you could pick up in your hand. Pepsi spent millions of dollars studying competitive designs. In 1958 they came up with the "swirl" bottle, but it never achieved the recognition of the Coca-Cola bottle. Eventually they solved the problem by a leap of the imagination which involved shifting the ground rules. They changed not the shape of the bottle but its size. They discovered in tests that no matter how much cola the shopper took home it was all consumed. So Pepsi manufactured large plastic bottles for supermarket sale rather than six packs or eight packs of smaller bottles. When Coca-Cola followed suit, they could not translate their valuable silhouette to the larger-sized plastic bottles. One of Coca-Cola's key competitive advantages had been wiped out.

Sometimes the great leap of the imagination comes about by chance. Sir Alexander Fleming discovered the

remarkably effective antibiotic penicillin when he noticed that a mould that had grown by chance on one of his laboratory plates was highly resistant to bacteria. Röntgen accidentally discovered X-rays while investigating electric-current flows in cathode ray tubes. Great scientists such as these and others were able to make great leaps by harnessing the creative power of a chance happening.

In the puzzles which follow, a leap of the imagination would definitely help. Use the techniques you have already learned regarding testing assumptions and asking the right questions. Then when you get stuck force yourself to try new lines of inquiry. Throw out the conventional and *think laterally*! This means more than just taking wild guesses. It means adopting a new approach, coming at the problem from a different direction, and being creative.

Skill Test 3

✦

3.1 The All-Night Party   POINT VALUE/50

In a small town in the United States a teenage boy asked his parents if he could go to a friend's party. His parents agreed, provided that he was back before sunrise. He left the house that evening clean-shaven and when he returned just before the following sunrise his parents were amazed to see that he had a fully grown beard. What happened?

3.2 The Approaching Constable   POINT VALUE/50

One evening two men were about to break into a shop front on a London street. Suddenly they heard someone approaching around the side of the building. "That is a constable coming," said one of the men. "Let's go!" They could not see who it was and they heard no sound other than footsteps, so how did the man know that it was a police officer approaching?

3.3 A Strange Habit   POINT VALUE/50

Tim was travelling through Europe. Every time he came to an airport he took off his shoes. Why?

3.4 The Climbing Bear   POINT VALUE/50

It has been noticed that bears often climb telegraph poles. Why do they do this?

3.5 Coconut Grove   POINT VALUE/60

An American nightclub called the Coconut Grove had a terrible fire in which over 400 people died. A simple design flaw in the building led to the death toll being so high. Subsequently, regulations were changed to ensure that all public buildings throughout the country eliminated this one detail which proved so deadly. What was it?

3.6 The Shriek   POINT VALUE/60

A woman dived into a swimming pool and then shrieked in horror. Why?

3.7 The Parking Ticket   POINT VALUE/60

John parked his car for three hours on a busy London street where no parking is allowed. An efficient traffic warden visited the street every hour and carefully gave a parking ticket to every car parked there. Although there was a ticket on John's car when he returned, he threw it away and never paid it. What is more, the authorities were unable to catch him for this, despite the fact that it was his car, displaying its correct registration. What had he done?

3.8 Death Sentence   POINT VALUE/60

A man in the United States decided that he would kill someone. Although he had not chosen exactly who it was who should die, he went to a court and obtained a court order allowing him to kill a person. The court order prevented him from being prosecuted. He then carried out the killing and no one tried to stop him. Can you explain?

3.9 The Tip-Off   POINT VALUE/70

A burglar broke into the house of an old lady and, while she was asleep, he robbed her of her life savings. When he got home he phoned the police and told them. Why?

3.10 The Lawsuit   POINT VALUE/70

The tallest building in a famous city is 62 storeys high and covered in glass panels. The proud owners of the new building were horrified when glass panels started to fall off the building, causing danger and damage in the surrounding area. It transpired that the glass manufacturer had been negligent in supplying glass which was not properly pre-stressed, as specified in the building designs. The company that owned the building instituted a lawsuit against the glass company claiming millions of dollars worth of damages. They had an excellent case and would have won the suit, but one week before it was due to start they dropped all claims against the glass company and received no compensation whatsoever. Why?

3.11 The Two Walkers   POINT VALUE/70

Two men were walking. One of them was carrying a bag which was very precious to them both. Suddenly they saw a stranger in the distance. They carefully hid the bag and rushed to meet the stranger. They never went back for the bag. Why not?

3.12 The Two Climbers   POINT VALUE/80

Alan and Barry were keen climbers. They would each have dearly loved to climb the city's cathedral spire but they knew that it would not be allowed by the authorities. The archbishop was a stickler for maintaining the appearance and dignity of his cathedral and he would not entertain the idea of allowing climbers to scale its spire for fun.

Alan proposed that they climb the spire in secret at night. Barry thought for a while and then declared that he had a better idea; he would secure the approval of the archbishop to climb the spire in broad daylight.

The next morning they knocked at the archbishop's door, secured his permission, and in full view of an admiring crowd climbed the spire. What was Barry's clever idea that persuaded the archbishop to agree?

3.13 The Two Fingers POINT VALUE/80

A man cut off the first and second fingers on the right hand of six other men. Why?

Clues

Each clue costs 10 points.

3.1 The All-Night Party

1. No potions, transplants, wigs or tricks are involved. It was the same boy and he returned before the next sunrise, having been out long enough to grow a proper beard.

3.2 The Approaching Constable

1. They could not see through or around the shop and there was no one else involved. There were no mirrors or cameras involved.

2. They did not hear anything that indicated the constable's presence, but they did see something.

3. It was a sunny evening.

3.3 A Strange Habit

1. Tim was a normal businessman. He had no criminal tendencies or physical disabilities. He took off his shoes to save himself trouble.

2. The reason for his action was connected with airport security. He took his shoes off for a few minutes only and then put them on again.

3.4 The Climbing Bear

1. The bears who climb telegraph poles do not do so out of fear but for a very deliberate reason. They make a wrong assumption.

2. If the poles were ordinary poles rather than telegraph poles, then the bears would not climb them.

3. They hear something which leads them to make a wrong assumption.

3.5 Coconut Grove

1. The problem did not concern ventilation, fire extinguishers, corridors, windows or inflammable building materials. It concerned the means of escape from the building.

2. The people who died were found piled up at the doors, where they had been suffocated by smoke and burned. Yet the doors were not locked and anyone could open them.

3.6 The Shriek

1. It was a regular swimming pool containing water. Other people were swimming safely there. The woman was a good swimmer and there was no physical danger to her in the pool.

2. She realized something as soon as she dived in. Immediately she knew that she should not have dived in. She was in perfect health and she suffered no physical injury.

3.7 The Parking Ticket

1. What he did was illegal. When he arrived, there were cars already there. He parked, knowing that a traffic warden would visit the street and see his car parked illegally. He did not have a doctor's sign, disabled sign, or any kind of dispensation.

2. The traffic warden ensured that every car parked illegally was given a ticket in the form of the official fine wrapped in plastic and stuck on the car's windshield. The traffic warden saw John's car.

3.8 Death Sentence

1. The man was a doctor. He had to kill one person so that another might live.

2. He had to choose one of two people to die. They were young and related.

3.9 The Tip-Off

1. The burglar did not phone the police to give them information about himself or the burglary. The old lady was ultimately pleased that the burglar spoke to the police.

2. The burglar had noticed something in the house which he recognized as a danger to the lady.

3. Although he took her money and jewels, the lady was pleased to see that he had left her antique brass doorstop.

3.10 The Lawsuit

1. The company that owned the building would have won the lawsuit but would have been worse off having won it. This was not because the legal fees would have been higher than the damages. They could expect damages of $10 million and legal fees of $1 million.

2. The company that owned the building did not own any part of the glass company. There were no ties because of people or families between the two companies. However, there was a commercial relationship between them.

3.11 The Two Walkers

1. The two men had been walking for a long time and they were very pleased to see the stranger. They had not seen anyone for a long time and they had thought that they would die.

2. The bag contained something that had helped them to survive but which they were now ashamed of.

3.12 The Two Climbers

1. Although the archbishop was opposed to anyone climbing the spire, the two climbers altered circumstances so that the archbishop was now pleased to allow them to climb the spire. They did not offer him money or publicity, but they did render him a useful service by climbing the spire.

2. The archbishop did not require them to take anything up the spire. By taking the action they did, they improved the appearance of the spire. The archbishop was pleased that they had climbed the spire and carried out the action they promised, but if he had known the whole truth he would have realized that he had been tricked.

3.13 The Two Fingers

1. The man who cut off the fingers was French. He was

not a criminal or a sadist. The six men who were his victims were all English.

2. The men who lost their fingers were prisoners of war. When they were captured they knew that they would probably lose their fingers.

3. The men who lost their fingers had all had a particular skill which they could now no longer practise.

Test 3 Score

Add your scores for the first *five* problems you tried. Then assess yourself against the following:

Grade A   Over 250 points—an excellent score
You have a creative and intelligent mind. You showed excellent imagination, flair, and clarity of thinking in solving the puzzles quickly. By now, your practice at checking assumptions and incisive questioning is also helping to make you a very good lateral thinker and puzzle solver.

Grade B   201 to 250 points—a very good score
Your creativity is good and your questioning technique allows you to accurately follow up new ideas. If you solved the puzzles without any clues, then your imagination is excellent but your questioning is still a little imprecise. If you got stuck at times and needed clues to help solve some of the puzzles, then the score shows that your questioning is good but there remains scope for you to be more open-minded and imaginative.

Grade C   141 to 200 points—an average score
Sometimes you show the imagination to make a breakthrough but often you get stuck, having run out of ideas and questions to ask. This is especially true if you

needed clues on most of the puzzles. Try to make a con-
scious effort to be more flexible and open-minded in
your approach to these kinds of problem and to everyday situations. Let your imagination off its leash and
come up with as many ideas as you can, however
"wacky." Testing lots of crazy ideas takes time and costs
points, but somewhere in there will be a lead to a breakthrough and the radical solution you need.

Grade D   Less than 140 points—a below-average score
If you failed to solve the problems despite getting all the
clues, then you need to analyze why. Are you being too
inhibited in your thinking? If you need to develop more
imaginative techniques, then you could practise brain-
storming, word association, and similar exercises in
building creativity. Go over some of the puzzles that
stumped you and try to figure out what blocked you
from seeing better lines of inquiry. If you are still making too many wrong assumptions or your questioning is
letting you down, then go over the key points in the
previous chapters. Try to take a more relaxed and
broad-minded approach.

4
Logical Thinking

❖ ❖ ❖

The Logical Approach

With all the foregoing emphasis on lateral and creative thinking and on discarding conventional approaches, it may seem a little strange to stress the benefits of logical thinking alongside lateral thinking. But to be first-class problem solvers we need to excel in both disciplines. Creative thinking and logical thinking should not be considered as alternatives but as complementary tools that we need in our problem-solving toolbox.

An example of a good logical thinker might be a lawyer who knows an enormous amount of detail on case history and legal precedent. In approaching a new case he can apply logic and a rational approach based on prior practice and experience to deduce the likely outcome. Because of his rational analyses of previous cases, he could advise the best line of defense or prosecution.

At the other extreme, an example of a good creative

thinker might be an advertising executive who comes up with ingenious and original ideas to meet tough marketing challenges. She would not be impressed by the conventional approach, what was tried in the past, or what the previous agency did. She would go back to first principles. She would not believe the conventional assumptions about her client's products but would test them using market research. Then she would come up with novel and imaginative ideas for solving the client's problem.

These expert professionals are skilfully using the different approaches of logical thinking and creative thinking to do their jobs well. But each would do the job even better if they were to add some of the other's skills.

If the lawyer could add some of the flair and creativity of the advertising executive he might come up with a really radical line of defense in a case which was very difficult to defend using conventional arguments.

If the advertising executive could apply some solid logic and analysis to her zany ideas, she could better select the one most likely to be a brilliant success. She could avoid the agony of proposing and implementing a fantastic concept which flopped in the harsh market of the real world.

Combining the open-minded, imaginative approach to problem solving with the skills of logical reasoning and analysis forms the basis of really successful lateral thinking.

A logical approach means using the information we have at hand to correctly deduce or figure out the answer. Of course, we still have to check our assumptions. We have to gather the right information by intelligent questioning. But once we have all the necessary information, we need to think it through in a clear and intelligent manner.

A concise but challenging logical-thinking puzzle goes

as follows: A man stands in front of a portrait and says, "Brothers and sisters have I none. But this man's father is my father's son."

Who is in the portrait? There is no trick in this question and you now have all the information you need to solve it, so stop reading, put down the book, and try to figure it out!

If we break the statement down into components we see that "my father's son" must be the man himself since he has no brothers. Therefore he is the father of the man in the portrait, and so the portrait is of his son.

In all the puzzles which follow you will have to use your powers of reasoning and deduction. They are pure reasoning problems, and since the statement of each puzzle contains all the information you need, no further questioning is allowed. You are allowed to use pencil and paper, of course, and if you get stuck there are clues, but each clue costs 10 points. To score points in these puzzles you have to figure out the complete solution.

Guesses (even correct ones) and incomplete solutions drop the score to zero. If you are stumped after 10 minutes on any one question you should give up, score zero, and go on to another. You should choose five problems.

Skill Test 4

✦

4.1 Pig Iron   POINT VALUE/50

A barge loaded with pig iron was in a lock. For some unknown reason the captain of the barge threw his iron overboard into the water. What happened to the water level in the lock?

4.2 Egg Timers   POINT VALUE/50

You have two traditional hourglass-type egg timers. One takes 7 minutes for the sand to run through, the other takes 11 minutes. You want to boil an ostrich egg for exactly 15 minutes. How can you do it? And how soon after the start of the whole process will the egg be ready? Needless to say, you want to consume the delicious ostrich egg as soon as possible.

4.3 Pour Away   POINT VALUE/50

A man went down to the river with two jugs, one of three-pint capacity and one of five-pint capacity. Using just these, how did he bring back exactly four pints?

4.4 The Explorer   POINT VALUE/50

An explorer wishes to cross a desolate desert on foot. It will take six days, but any one man can take enough food and water for four days only. Fortunately the local village can supply him with men who will act as bearers, but they charge $100 per day for their arduous work. What is the least number of bearers he needs to help him to make the journey, and what will it cost him in wages? (N.B.: Funeral costs for bearers are $1,000 each, so inhumane solutions are inadmissible!)

4.5 Water Transfer   POINT VALUE/50

There are two glasses of equal size, A and B. A is empty and B contains some water. Half the water in B is poured into A. This is repeated twice more—each time half of what is left in B is poured into A. At the end of these three pourings A is half full. How much water is now left in B?

4.6 Husbands and Wives   POINT VALUE/50

Three married couples, the Smiths, the Joneses, and the Browns, were sitting in a row of six chairs. No one sat next to a member of his or her own sex. Mrs. Smith was second in the row and Mrs. Jones was not sixth. Only one married couple sat next to each other. Who were they?

4.7 The Sale   POINT VALUE/60

A man went to a sale and bought some plates at $5 each, some spoons at $1 each, and some beads at 5 cents each. He bought 100 items in total and spent exactly $100. On his way home he dropped a bead. How many of each did he buy?

4.8 The Oldest Likes Chocolate   POINT VALUE/60

The following conversation took place between an official at the Social Security office and a claimant for child benefits:

"How many children do you have?"
"Three."
"What are their ages?"
"The product of their ages is 36."
"You will have to give me more information."
"The sum of their ages equals the number of the shop opposite this office."

"That is still not enough."

"That's right. The oldest child likes chocolate."

What were their ages?

4.9 Cutting the Cake   POINT VALUE/60

How could you cut a plain circular cake into eight equal portions with just three straight cuts of a knife? No rearrangement of the pieces after cutting is allowed.

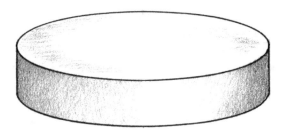

4.10 Battle of the Sexes   POINT VALUE/70

In the despotic state of Roxobia the government passed a decree which was aimed at reducing the population while increasing the number of boys available for military service. It stated that every family must stop having children as soon as a girl was born. So, if a couple's first child was a girl, then no more children were allowed. If a couple had ten boys, they could keep on having children until a girl arrived. This law was rigorously enforced. If the chances of having a boy and girl are equal, will there eventually be more boys than girls or more girls than boys? Did the government succeed in its two objectives?

4.11 A Crowded Crypt   POINT VALUE/70

In a certain old churchyard deep in rural England there is the following inscription on a crypt:

Here lie:
  Two grandmothers with their two granddaughters,
  Two husbands with their two wives,
  Two mothers with their two sons,
  Two fathers with their two daughters,
  And two maidens with their two mothers.
  Yet only six people are buried here.

Given that these statements were true, that none of the relationships described was an in-law relationship, and that there was no incest, can you explain it?

4.12 An Age-Old Problem   POINT VALUE/70

The philosophy lecturer asked the math lecturer how old his children were. He was given this enigmatic reply: "John is twice as old as Jane was when he was as old as she is now. The sum of their ages is 63." Thereupon, the philosophy lecturer nodded sagely. How old were the two children?

4.13 Strained Relations   POINT VALUE/80

Sam and Pat were having a talk. Said Sam to Pat, "I am the same relation to Bobby that Bobby is to you." Pat replied to Sam, "Yes, and I am the same relation to you that Bobby is to your father." What was the relationship between Sam and Pat?

Clues

Each clue costs 10 points.

4.1 Pig Iron

1. The water level can either go up, go down, or remain the same, but a guess is not good enough here. There are two different effects to think about. Once the iron is thrown out it makes the boat lighter; it also displaces some water when it is in the water.

4.2 Egg Timers

1. How can you time 11 minutes on the 11-minute timer and 4 minutes on the 7-minute timer in the shortest possible time after starting?

4.3 Pour Away

1. This really is much easier than it at first appears and can be solved in more than one way. Try to work backwards from what the final action must be. He could either add 3 pints from the 3 jug to 1 pint already in the 5 jug or he could empty exactly 1 pint out of a full 5 jug.

4.4 The Explorer

1. A man can carry four days' supplies, and if he turns back after one day he can pass on two days' supplies to two other men, leaving one day's supply for his return.

4.5 Water Transfer

1. However much water was in glass B to start, half is left after one pouring, one quarter is left after two pourings, and one eighth is left after three pourings. So seven-eighths has been transferred.

4.6 Husbands and Wives

1. Since Mrs. Jones is not sixth in the row she must be fourth. That means that Mrs. Brown must be sixth. Now start trying to figure out where Mr. Brown can sit.

4.7 The Sale

1. He definitely bought at least one bead. The number of beads he bought must be a multiple of 20; otherwise the total bill would not amount to an even number of dollars. So, he must have gotten either 20, 40, 60, or 80 beads. Work through the possibilities.

4.8 The Oldest Likes Chocolate

1. If you multiply the ages of the children together, then you get 36. It follows that the eldest child must have an age of either 36, 18, 12, 9, or 6. Bear in mind that two of his three children might be twins.

2. If you have correctly calculated the possible combinations of the ages of the children, then you will know that two of the combinations have the same sum.

4.9 Cutting the Cake

1. You make three straight cuts while the cake remains in place. The first two cuts are rather obvious and the third is very lateral!

4.10 Battle of the Sexes

1. Compared to a normal population there will be fewer large families because any family starting with a girl stops there. There will be some large families containing only boys, or several boys and then one girl. But to figure out the exact effect of that on the total population requires you to model a small but typical example.

2. Try drawing a tree diagram showing what happens to a sample set of families. Half of them stop after one daughter. The rest have a son. Some will stop there, but others will go on to have larger families. At each stage the chance of the next child being a boy or girl will be equal. So do the large families of several boys and one girl matter?

4.11 A Crowded Crypt

1. There are four women and two men buried in the vault. Each man has a mother, a wife, and a daughter there.

2. A widow can marry another woman's son.

4.12 An Age-Old Problem

1. If their ages are x and y (x being John's), then the difference in their ages is x − y. So John's age, x, is twice what Jane's was x − y years ago.

4.13 Strained Relations

1. Sam, Pat, and Bobby are all male humans. There are no step relations or in-law relations involved. The relationships are blood relationships.

2. Since they are all male, the relationships between them must be either father and son, uncle and nephew, or brothers. If we test these possibilities in turn, we find that two of them are impossible. The exact relationship is then found either with very strict logic or a little trial and error.

Test 4 Score

Add your scores for the first *five* problems you tried. Then assess yourself against the following:

Grade A   Over 230 points—an excellent score

You have a very logical and analytical mind. If you can couple this with creativity and imagination, then you have the perfect combination of attributes for lateral thinking. By now you will also know how good you are at questioning and testing assumptions. If you have scored well in this logical thinking section but did poorly in previous sections, then you are a logical rather than a lateral thinker. If you move to the next section you can compute your overall score.

Grade B   181 to 230 points—a very good score

Your logic and reasoning are good. Maintaining a solid balance of skills between logic, reasoning, questioning, and imagination is the aim in good lateral thinking. Work on this balance.

Grade C   131 to 180 points—an average score

Your reasoning skills are good but could be better. Do you shy away from numerical analysis and focus more on literal or creative skills? To be a true lateral thinker you need some numerical, analytical, and logical skills, so it could be worthwhile concentrating on improving these areas. Go back to the puzzles which stumped you and go through them. Do you still find them difficult, or do they seem straightforward once explained? If you followed all the logic but did not apply it, then it may be that your brain needs more exercise in this area! Try doing more number and logic puzzles in newspapers and magazines.

Grade D   Less than 130 points—a below-average score

See the comments above, which apply even more strongly in your case. If you did not like the logical-type questions, and really detested the numerical ones, then you are probably better suited to a creative role in a team where you have an analytical and logical colleague to help you to build solutions. On the other hand, you could be logical about this, and point out that five puzzles are not a statistically valid sample and that this result was an aberration!

Overall Scoring

Your Lateral-Thinking Profile

If you have shown the persistence and fortitude to do all four tests and record your scores, then well done! We can now assess two things.

The first is your lateral-thinking profile. This shows how you did in each of the tests and whether you improved as you went through the book.

Review your scores and plot your progress on a graph like this one:

PROFILE CHART

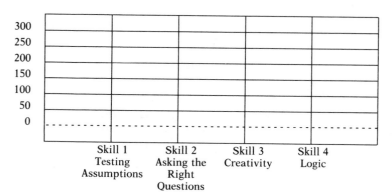

If your scores show an upward trend, then you have learned some useful techniques and the testing was of value. It would indeed be surprising if your questioning technique, in particular, had not improved. However, if your score did decline as you went along, then you can console yourself with the assurance that the puzzles became harder.

The kind of profile which would indicate good aptitude at lateral thinking would start with a Skill 1 score of 150-plus and then show average scores of over 200.

We can also use the Profile Chart to assess the balance of your lateral-thinking skills. To be a really good lateral thinker you need an A or B grade (over 200) in each of the four key skills: Testing Assumptions, Questioning, Creativity, and Logical Thinking. If your scores in these sections are unbalanced, then you know which areas need to be focused on for improvement.

Overall Score Assessment

Finally, we can calculate your overall score. Add your scores from the five problems you did in each of the four main sections: Testing Assumptions, Asking the Right Questions, Creativity, and Logical Thinking. Then assess your overall rating:

Over 1,000 points	A truly outstanding lateral thinker
851 to 1,000 points	A very good lateral thinker
701 to 850 points	A good lateral thinker
551 to 700 points	An average lateral thinker
401 to 550 points	An enthusiast who, with improvement, will become a lateral thinker
Less than 400 points	Someone who did the tests just for fun!

Put Your Lateral
Thinking to Work

✦ ✦ ✦

If you are riding a horse that suddenly bolts, then there are a number of possible actions you can take. One would be to pull harder and harder on the reins. This is the conventional thinking approach—it involves using the same methods which you were taught when learning to ride and which have proved effective up until now. But if the horse is in a wild panic, then the conventional approach will not work no matter how hard you pull. Another solution could be to cover the horse's eyes with your hands. This is the lateral thinking approach—a radically different but effective solution.

Examples of lateral thinking, such as the arch replacing the lintel, or the Fosbury flop replacing the western roll, or Arabic numbering superseding Roman numerals, or controlling a bolting horse by covering its eyes, all involve similar principles. In each case the well-known, proven, regular method of solving the problem is replaced not by extension or development but by a completely new solution.

The key elements of lateral thinking are testing assumptions, a questioning process which systematically

sifts for the right information, the creative use of imagination, and, finally, logical analysis. Or rather, not finally, because there are other aspects of lateral thinking
which lie outside the scope of this book. The four techniques we have presented, discussed, and tested are the
key tools for arriving at solutions. In real life, however,
there are no answers at the back of the book. So, the true
lateral thinker takes his or her proposed solution and
then implements it, tests it, analyzes the results, and
learns from that experience. Thinking of a solution is
everything in solving book puzzles, but in real-life problems it is only half the battle. The other half is effective
implementation of the solution. A good lateral thinker is
also a doer, an experimenter, a trier, an adapter, and a
learner.

As a lateral thinker you boldly implement your best
ideas. Then you carefully analyze the results and feed-
back. You examine what happened as a result of the
change and then take appropriate corrective action. The
proper management of change is usually a continuous
process.

At an individual level this can be exciting and attain-
able. At an organization-wide level the management of
the change process initiated by lateral thinking can be
very difficult and demand significant time and skill. This
is needed to communicate enthusiasm for the change to
all levels and to overcome the inevitable resistance of
vested interests. The more radical and lateral the
change, the greater the resistance is likely to be. Really
large organizations are particularly resistant to fundamental innovation. A change affecting the whole orga-
nization can be achieved only with the enthusiastic and
visible commitment of its leaders.

However difficult the management of change may be,
only those organizations which master the process will
survive. Since the rate of change in our society is accel-

erating, those who can master change and drive it will be the winners, those who stand back or instinctively resist it will be the losers. The age of change will result in a greater and greater demand for those who can think laterally, who can adapt, who can question all previous assumptions and ground rules, who can come up with creative new solutions that are properly thought through and who can then implement them, either singly or in teams.

The need for teaching and improving lateral thinking abilities has never been greater. The lateral thinking puzzles on which we train our minds may be small and fun, but the challenges in society for which we need these skills are immense and serious. For most of these problems, just pulling harder on the reins is not good enough.

Puzzle Answers

✦ ✦ ✦

1 Testing Assumptions

1.1 The Secretary's Daughter

The secretary was the girl's father.

1.2 Pizza

At 11 p.m. every Thursday evening a police officer (in uniform) would come into the pizza parlor and place a particular order, which the night shift at the local station then shared. One Thursday evening the man in plain clothes came and placed the same regular order.

1.3 The Fishermen's Riddle

The two fishermen were talking about their fleas!

1.4 The Barber Paradox

The conventional answer to this problem is that it is a circular paradox. If he shaves himself, then he breaks the law, and if he doesn't, he breaks the law. However, the lateral thinking answer is that the issue does not arise—no one shaves the licensed town barber as she is a woman!

1.5 Late Arrival

They had been talking about the girl's birth.

1.6 Watch That Movie

The movie was shown twice on the flight, once before lunch and once after lunch. Hugh watched it the first time and was therefore not interested the second time.

1.7 The Cabin

It is a plane cabin. The plane crashed, killing both pilots and the passenger.

1.8 The Unkind Cut

The man was imprisoned in the notorious Devil's Island penal colony. Over a period of months he cut off fingers and an ear and he feigned numbness in a leg in order to pretend that he had leprosy. He was then transferred to a different island which held only lepers. It was much easier to escape from this island and he duly made his getaway and reached Brazil. Unfortunately (for this is a true story) he was subsequently found to have developed leprosy.

1.9 The Triangles Death

The man had been caught cheating at cards. The 52 triangles were on the backs of his marked deck.

1.10 The Soldier

The German soldier and his small group had been surrounded by the Russian partisans and eventually only he and his younger brother were left alive. Knowing what terrible things the partisans did to captured Germans, he had used his last bullet to shoot his brother.

1.11 The Bird

He saw a big heron in the tree over his ornamental pond and guessed (correctly) that it had eaten his large and valuable koi carp.

1.12 The Bank Manager

He was flying from New York to Switzerland for an important meeting. He wore the face-mask to exclude the light so that he could sleep on the flight.

1.13 The Fish

The man was under a death threat because he had been a prosecution witness in a Mafia trial. In order to escape he had been given a different identity and had set up a new life for himself. The sending of a dead fish is a traditional Mafia death threat. When he received the dead fish in the mail, the man knew that the Mafia had uncovered his identity and that he would surely be killed.

2 Asking the Right Questions

2.1 Luigi's

Luigi's restaurant is on board ship.

2.2 What a Drive!

The four states are Arizona, New Mexico, Utah and Colorado, which meet at a single point. A pipe was set up there in the form of a large circle, placed so that it lay in all four states. A well-struck golf ball entering the pipe would travel through the four states.

2.3 Tall Buildings

The Japanese insurance company believes strongly in physical fitness and that going up and down stairs keeps its employees healthier and more alert. No employee is allowed to use the elevator, or lift, unless she or he has a medical certificate!

2.4 The Broken Bag

This unfortunate woman was a drug courier or "mule." She had swallowed numerous condoms filled with heroin before boarding a flight for London. One condom split inside her and she died from a massive overdose.

2.5 A Veiled Threat

The woman was a beekeeper who unfortunately knocked over a hive. The bees swarmed all over her. She was thrown into the pool to save her from their attacks, but it was too late—she was stung to death.

2.6 The Unexpected Kiss

The man had an identical twin brother with whom the lady had recently fallen in love.

2.7 The Legacy

The man and his father were keen stamp collectors. The inner envelope had a rare stamp on it worth $20,000.

2.8 By the Pool

He had jumped from his hotel balcony to escape a fire raging through the hotel. He had wrapped a towel around his face to help him breathe through the smoke and he had leapt for the pool but missed by inches.

2.9 The Fisherman

A national border ran across the lake. The southeastern part of the lake was in another country, which was considerably more repressive and unfriendly than the homeland of the fisherman. Anyone crossing the border without all the necessary prior authorization was considered a spy and would be shot by the border guards.

2.10 Food for Thought

The Danish government issues dog biscuits to all its postal delivery people every morning so that they can use them to distract hostile dogs.

2.11 Cheap Treasure

The item was a car number plate containing the woman's name in its letters.

2.12 The Train Problem

John got on the front of his train. During the two-minute wait for the next train Bill walked the length of the platform and got on at the back of the train. When Bill got off his train he met John, who had just spent two minutes walking down the platform after alighting from his train.

2.13 Lost Jewelry

In this true incident, the wife had hidden her best jewelry inside her freezer in a bag among all the frozen food. Because of a general power failure the freezer had gone off. A friendly neighbor (who had a key in order to water the plants) had tried to be helpful by throwing out all the bad food—and with it went the jewelry.

3 Creativity

3.1 The All-Night Party

The small town was Barrow in Alaska, the northernmost town in the United States. When the sun sets there in the middle of November, it does not rise again for 65 days. That allowed plenty of time for the boy to grow a beard before the next sunrise.

3.2 The Approaching Constable

English police officers wear distinctive high helmets. One of the men saw the shadow of the individual approaching and realized that it must be a police officer from the shape of the shadow cast by the helmet.

3.3 A Strange Habit

Tim was wearing shoes with steel buckles. He removed them every time he came to a security-check machine so as not to set it off.

3.4 The Climbing Bear

The bear hears the wires humming and mistakes this for bees humming. It climbs the telegraph pole in search of honey in the beehive.

3.5 Coconut Grove

The doors at the Coconut Grove opened inward. In the mad panic to escape the fire, people were crushed against the doors and could not pull them open. After the Coconut Grove disaster in 1942, all public buildings had to have doors which opened outward.

3.6 The Shriek

She realized that she was still wearing the new gold watch which her husband had given her for their silver wedding anniversary. It was not waterproof.

3.7 The Parking Ticket

When John parked his car, there were some other illegally parked cars in the street. He simply took a ticket from one of their windshields and stuck it on his own. This is, of course, completely illegal, but it did mean that no ticket was ever written for his car and he could not be traced.

3.8 Death Sentence

In this true case the man was a doctor who had to operate to separate seven-week-old Siamese twins who shared the same heart. One had to die to give the other a chance to live.

3.9 The Tip-Off

This incident happened a few years ago in northeast France. The burglar noticed that the old lady's brass doorstop was an unexploded World War I shell. He phoned the police to alert them to the danger.

3.10 The Lawsuit

The company that owned the building was an insurance group. They discovered late in the proceedings that one of their companies carried the insurance coverage for the glass company's liability. So if they had won the suit, they would have had to bear the ultimate cost of compensating themselves!

3.11 The Two Walkers

The scene is taken from the true story *Alive* by Piers Paul Read concerning the survivors of a plane which crashed in a valley high in the Andes. Without food, the survivors were forced to eat their dead companions. Eventually two of them climbed out of the desolate valley and after walking for days reached civilization in Chile. They carried a precious supply of food—dried human meat. When they at last saw someone, they buried the bag and never returned for it.

3.12 The Two Climbers

They secretly climbed the spire the night before and left a gaudy kite lodged at the top. When they called on the archbishop the following morning, they pointed out that a kite was stuck on the spire and offered to climb the structure in order to remove this eyesore. The archbishop happily agreed to their helpful offer!

3.13 The Two Fingers

The men who lost their fingers were English archers. During the Hundred Years War between France and England, English archers using their longbows posed a significant military threat to the French. They were largely responsible for the English victory at the battle of Agincourt in 1415. The French declared that any English archer who was caught would have his index and second finger cut off, thereby incapacitating him. The Frenchman who cut off the six men's fingers was simply carrying out this instruction. Incidentally, English archers often waved their two fingers at French opponents as a sign of derision. This is the source of the gesture which is still used to this day.

4 Logical Thinking

4.1 Pig Iron

The water level in the lock went down. When the iron was in the barge it displaced its own weight of water, but when it was thrown overboard it displaced its own volume of water—which would be much less. To put it another way, because the boat was lighter it rode much higher in the water, causing the water level to go down.

4.2 Egg Timers

There are a number of ways of doing this; the quickest takes just 15 minutes from the start. Start both timers together. When the 7-minute timer is finished, turn it over immediately. It will then run for 4 minutes before the 11-minute timer finishes. Turn the 7-minute timer over again at that point and it will measure a further 4 minutes; i.e., 15 minutes in total.

4.3 Pour Away

Answer A: He filled the 3 jug from the 5 jug, leaving 2 pints in the 5 jug. He emptied the 3 jug and then poured the 2 pints from the 5 jug into the 3 jug. He then refilled the 5 jug and from it he filled the 3 jug, leaving exactly 4 pints in his 5 jug.

Answer B: He filled the 3 jug and then poured it into the 5 jug. He refilled the 3 jug and from it filled the 5 jug, leaving 1 pint in the 3 jug. He emptied the 5 jug and then poured the 1 pint from the 3 jug into the 5 jug. He refilled the 3 jug and poured it into the 5 jug, making 4 pints exactly in the 5 jug.

4.4 The Explorer

He needs only two bearers. The first goes with him for only one day and then returns, having handed over one day's supply to each of the other two men. The second bearer carries on a second day and then hands one day's supply to the explorer before returning. The explorer then has four days' supply for the remaining four days' journey.

The first man gets two days' wages and the second gets four, so it costs the explorer $600.

4.5 Water Transfer

If the original amount of water in B is X, then the amount transferred is:

$$\frac{1}{2}X + \frac{1}{4}X + \frac{1}{8}X = \frac{7}{8}X$$
$$\text{So } \frac{7}{8}X = \text{half a glass}$$
$$X = \frac{4}{7} \text{ of a glass}$$

and the amount remaining in B is $\frac{1}{14}$ of a glass.

4.6 Husbands and Wives

Mr. and Mrs. Jones sat next to each other.

4.7 The Sale

He bought 19 plates, 1 spoon, and 80 beads.

4.8 The Oldest Likes Chocolate

If all the answers are correct, then this infuriating claimant has three children whose ages when multiplied together make 36. The possibilities therefore are:

Ages			Sum
36	1	1	38
18	2	1	21
12	3	1	16
9	4	1	14
9	2	2	13
6	6	1	13
6	3	2	11
4	3	3	10

When the official was given the second piece of information, the shop number, he said that this was still insufficient. So the sum of the ages must have been 13—the only sum for which there are two possible sets of ages. Since the oldest likes chocolate, it follows that the answer is 9, 2, and 2.

4.9 Cutting the Cake

With the first two cuts you divide the cake from the top into quarters. You then take the knife and slice (laterally) through the middle of the side of the cake.

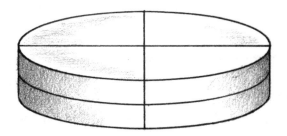

4.10 Battle of the Sexes

The nasty government succeeded in reducing the population, but its autocratic decree had no effect on the balance of boys and girls. The population was reduced because every couple whose first child was a girl had to stop. Some of them would normally have had larger families.

On the other hand, because the chances for any birth are exactly equal, the overall numbers of boys and girls will be equal. The only way that the government could increase the proportion of boys born would be to increase the likelihood that any birth would be a boy.

To test this, try working out what happens if there are 64 couples who would all like to have four children (say) and who all follow the government's rules. So 32 couples stop after one girl; 32 carry on after a first boy. Of those 32, 16 stop after boy–girl and 16 carry on after boy–boy. If you carry on with the process, you will find that the numbers of boys and girls are exactly equal at 60 each. (It does not alter the matter if a certain proportion of families stop after only having had boys.)

4.11 A Crowded Crypt

There were two widows who each had a son. Each widow married the son of the other widow and each marriage produced one daughter. The daughters were each, therefore, the granddaughter of one widow and the daughter of the other. When these six people were buried together, the relationships described were correct.

4.12 An Age-Old Problem

John is 36 and Jane is 27 years old.

4.13 Strained Relations

Sam is Pat's grandfather. Bobby is Sam's son and Pat's father.

Index

About the Author

Paul Sloane was born in Scotland and grew up near Blackpool in the north of England. He studied engineering at Trinity Hall, Cambridge, and graduated with a first-class honors degree. While at Cambridge he met his wife, who is a teacher. They live in Camberley, England, with their three daughters.

Most of Paul Sloane's career has been in the computer industry and he is currently the European vice-president for a software company. He has always been an avid collector and creator of puzzles. His first book, *Lateral Thinking Puzzlers*, was published by Sterling in 1991, and two other such puzzle books, co-authored with colleague Des MacHale, followed. Paul Sloane has also given talks on change management and lateral thinking.